Thomas Jefferson

*Author of the Declaration
of Independence*

Colonial Leaders

Lord Baltimore *English Politician and Colonist*

Benjamin Banneker *American Mathematician and Astronomer*

William Bradford *Governor of Plymouth Colony*

Benjamin Franklin *American Statesman, Scientist, and Writer*

Anne Hutchinson *Religious Leader*

Cotton Mather *Author, Clergyman, and Scholar*

William Penn *Founder of Democracy*

John Smith *English Explorer and Colonist*

Miles Standish *Plymouth Colony Leader*

Peter Stuyvesant *Dutch Military Leader*

Revolutionary War Leaders

Benedict Arnold *Traitor to the Cause*

Nathan Hale *Revolutionary Hero*

Alexander Hamilton *First U.S. Secretary of the Treasury*

Patrick Henry *American Statesman and Speaker*

Thomas Jefferson *Author of the Declaration of Independence*

John Paul Jones *Father of the U.S. Navy*

Thomas Paine *Political Writer*

Paul Revere *American Patriot*

Betsy Ross *American Patriot*

George Washington *First U.S. President*

Thomas Jefferson

Author of the Declaration of Independence

Veda Boyd Jones

Arthur M. Schlesinger, jr.
Senior Consulting Editor

Chelsea House Publishers

Philadelphia

Produced by 21st Century Publishing and Communications, Inc.
New York, NY. http://www.21cpc.com

CHELSEA HOUSE PUBLISHERS
Editor in Chief Stephen Reginald
Production Manager Pamela Loos
Director of Photography Judy L. Hasday
Art Director Sara Davis
Managing Editor James D. Gallagher

Staff for *THOMAS JEFFERSON*
Project Editor/Publishing Coordinator Jim McAvoy
Associate Art Director Takeshi Takahashi
Series Design Keith Trego

The Chelsea House World Wide Web address is
http://www.chelseahouse.com

First Printing
1 3 5 7 9 8 6 4 2

Library of Congress Cataloging-in-Publication Data

Jones, Veda Boyd.
Thomas Jefferson / by Veda Boyd Jones.
80 pp. cm. — (Revolutionary War Leaders series)
Includes bibliographical references and index.
Summary: A biography of the multitalented leader who wrote the
Declaration of Independence and became the third president of the
United States, discussing his childhood, education, involvement in
colonial politics, writings, and career as a statesman.
ISBN 0-7910-5353-9 (hc)   ISBN 0-7910-5696-1 (pb)
1. Jefferson, Thomas, 1743-1826—Juvenile literature. 2. Presidents—
United States—Biography—Juvenile literature. 3. Statesmen—United
States—Biography—Juvenile literature. 4. United States—History—
Revolution, 1775-1783—Biography—Juvenile literature. [1. Jefferson,
Thomas, 1743-1826. 2. Presidents.] I. Title. II. Series.
E332.79.J66 1999
973.4'6'—dc21   99-20693
[B]   CIP

Publisher's Note: In Colonial and Revolutionary War America,
there were no standard rules for spelling, punctuation, capitaliza-
tion, or grammar. Some of the quotations that appear in the Colonial Leaders and Revolutionary War Leaders series come from
original documents and letters written during this time in history.
Original quotations reflect writing inconsistencies of the period.

Contents

Thomas Jefferson grew up on a plantation in Virginia called Shadwell. Most plantations grew tobacco to sell and other crops for food. They also raised livestock and often lived very far from their neighbors.

Life on the Plantation

The red-haired baby let out a loud sustained squall when he came into the world. He was quite long, which was a sign that he would be a very tall man. The boy was given the name Thomas Jefferson.

He was born in the wilderness of the Virginia **colony** on April 13, 1743. Virginia was not a state at that time because the United States had not been formed yet. Britain, a country far across the Atlantic Ocean, controlled the colony. Britain was ruled by a king and, therefore, the king of Britain also ruled the colony.

Thomas's parents lived on a **plantation** on the frontier. It was called Shadwell, after a place in Britain. Sometimes Thomas's father, Peter, would take him for a horseback ride on their land, riding into the woods and across the river. At one edge of their land was a small mountain. From the top they could see the peaks of the larger Blue Ridge Mountains.

Peter Jefferson was a big strong man, and he was very smart. He liked to read, and he liked to work outside in the fresh air. He worked as a **surveyor** and drew maps.

Few people lived on the frontier, but many Native Americans roamed throughout this area. Sometimes the Indians camped at Shadwell. Peter was friendly with Indians and with settlers. He was also friendly with rich farmers in the area by the big rivers. His best friend was William Randolph. The two men promised each other that if one of them died, the other one would take care of his friend's family and land. William Randolph died when Thomas was

Thomas's father, like other colonists, often traded with the Indians. He was friendly with both the Indians and the settlers who lived along the frontier.

just three years old. Thomas's father kept his promise to his friend, and he moved the family 50 miles away to the large Randolph plantation, to better take care of William's family.

Thomas and his two older sisters went to a

little school in the side yard with the Randolph children. By the time he was five, Thomas could read. He enjoyed learning. He loved books, and he liked to write down his thoughts about many things. But he did not like to speak in front of the class. He would speak very softly, and his voice could barely be heard.

When Thomas was nine years old, his father moved his family back to Shadwell. There was no school nearby for Thomas to attend. So his father decided to send him away to a boarding school. Thomas lived at the boarding school with his teacher. For five years he studied and learned many languages, including Latin and Greek. Thomas liked French best of all and became very good at speaking the language. He also taught himself to speak Italian and learned some German and Spanish.

Each summer Thomas returned to Shadwell and his family. His father taught him to ride a horse, and he felt as if he were riding as fast as the wind. Peter taught him to shoot a gun and hunt wild turkeys and deer. He also learned from his father how to paddle a canoe on the river. Thomas looked up to his father, who was a leader in the area. At different times his father had served as sheriff, judge, justice of the peace, and as a member of the Virginia **House of Burgesses**. This was the group of men who made laws for the colony. Thomas knew his father was smart, and he wanted to be like him.

Many times each summer Thomas climbed to the top of the little mountain on the edge of the family's land and looked across at the great Blue Ridge Mountains. He often wondered what lay on the other side of the vast mountain range. His father told him it was a wild place that didn't have roads for wagons or many paths for horses.

When Thomas was 14 years old, his father died. By that time Thomas had six sisters and a brother. In his will, Thomas's father left something to all his children, but since Thomas

Young Thomas was filled with curiosity about the plants and animals in the wilderness around his home. He often rode his horse into the woods to study them and make notes about what he saw.

was the oldest boy, he received the most. His father knew how much learning meant to Thomas, so he left Thomas his books, his desk, his bookcase, his math instruments, and a slave. When Thomas turned 21 he was to receive many more slaves and more than 2,500 acres of land.

After his father's death, Thomas lived at a different school. It was about 14 miles from Shadwell. In the log schoolhouse Thomas learned about history and literature. He was taught more Greek and Latin. He was eager to learn about many subjects. His teacher talked to him about government. Who should make laws? Only men who owned land or all the people? Thomas decided that all people should have a vote in government.

However, most of Thomas's schooling was not from books. His teacher took him and the other students on long hikes through the Blue Ridge Mountains. They searched for fossils. They looked at the many types of plants that grew there. They counted the different types of birds that lived in the forests. The class also learned to dance, and Thomas learned to play the violin.

Thomas was curious about almost everything he saw. Every day he wrote down what the temperature was outside. When he shot a tree squirrel on a hunting trip, he would see how much it weighed and write that down too. He wanted to compare and see if red, gray, and black squirrels all weighed the same.

On Saturdays he went home to be with his family. Many times he took his school friend Dabney Carr home with him. They took their horses out for long rides together, and often they chased after deer. Sitting under a huge oak tree on the little mountain, they talked seriously about what they each wanted be when they grew older. They made a promise to one another—when one of them died, the

Thomas had a very active and creative mind and he invented many different things during his lifetime. His dumbwaiter, a small elevator, carried wine from the cellar. His quartet music stand held sheets of music on four sides. His clever and practical polygraph machine allowed him to write his correspondence with one pen while a second attached pen made an exact copy for him to keep for his records. Thomas's swivel chair design is still copied today.

other one would make sure he was buried under that tree.

By the time Thomas was 16, he decided to go to college. He had learned a lot from his teacher. But he wanted to meet more people and see more of the world. At 17 Thomas was accepted at the College of William and Mary, which was in Williamsburg, the capital of Virginia. In the spring of 1760, he traveled to the college. He was a country boy, and for him, going to the city was like going to an amazing whole new world.

Williamsburg was the capital city of the Virginia colony. To a young man from the country, like Thomas, it was an amazing sight with its people, buildings, and the governor's grand palace.

City Life

Thomas Jefferson had never seen a place as huge as Williamsburg. More than 200 houses stood on wide streets. Over 1,500 people lived in the busy city. For a boy from the frontier this was an awesome sight. Many stores lined the main street. There was a wigmaker's shop, a gunsmith's shop, and a candlemaker's store. Next to the jeweler's shop was the Raleigh Tavern. College students spent idle hours there talking, drinking, and playing cards.

A few blocks away stood the British governor's palace. At the end of the main street sat the stately capitol. The Virginia House of Burgesses met there. Most were wealthy men. When they came to town twice a year to meet in the capitol, they wanted to be entertained. They watched different stage plays and danced at festive balls. Often they would bet on horse races and card games or ride horses and go hunting. Whenever possible they ate very fancy dinners and drank fine wine and ale at the then well-know Raleigh Tavern.

Thomas wanted to be a part of all this excitement. He found that he was well ahead of most of his classmates in their college studies. Since schoolwork was so easy for him, he often headed to town after classes. He liked to go to the Raleigh Tavern and listen to the talk of the day. Many very important issues of government were being discussed there.

Since Thomas was fairly wealthy, he found he could buy things at stores on credit by just signing his name, and a bill would be sent to him later. His worn and rugged country clothes

Colonists often met in taverns to get the latest news and talk about politics and business. Thomas liked to go to the Raleigh Tavern in Williamsburg to hear the discussions.

weren't fine enough for Williamsburg, so he had new clothes made. He also kept a couple of horses with him so he could go riding or hunting with his friends whenever he wanted.

He made many good friends among the people. They liked the tall, red-haired, freckle-faced young man. He had fine manners and was a good dancer. He was invited to many homes for dinners.

One of Thomas's good friends was Patrick Henry. Patrick was seven years older than Thomas, and they were very different. Patrick was also from the country, but he dressed in buckskin instead of city clothes. He was a lawyer. To become a lawyer, a man needed to read law books and work in another lawyer's office for many years to learn the trade. Most men studied law for several years before they took the test to become a lawyer. Patrick read the law books in only six weeks, and he passed the test on his first try. He soon became a lawyer. Because he was such a good speaker, Patrick could make people believe what he believed with his fiery speeches.

Thomas admired Patrick, and whenever Patrick came to town, the two talked for long hours. They talked about government and law and the natural rights of man. They agreed on many important matters.

By the end of his first year at college, Thomas was surprised to discover how much money he had spent. He felt that he had not learned as much as he should have. Thomas decided to spend more time studying. Now he became quite serious about his studies. He took long and detailed notes as he listened to his instructors in class, and he also wrote down many notes when he read his books. He believed that if he wrote down the information, he would remember it better. If he did forget, he could look at his paper and recall it.

Professor William Small taught mathematics and philosophy at the college. He became a father figure to Thomas. When Thomas was tempted to go to town for a horse race or some other excitement, Dr. Small would ask Thomas to take a long walk with him to discuss Greek thinkers or some other subject. Thomas wanted to please Dr. Small, so he almost always went with him. Thomas was also glad to have the

Thomas studied Greek, Latin, mathematics, and philosophy at the College of William and Mary. When he graduated he became an assistant to his lawyer friend George Wythe.

opportunity to learn even more from such a highly educated man. Most days he studied for 14 hours. He still went to dances and dinners and parties, but he would often leave early to get back to his books.

Dr. Small introduced Thomas to lawyer

George Wythe, as well as to British Governor Francis Fauquier, who was sent by the king of England to run Virginia. Although the three men were much older than Thomas, they liked him and included him in many dinner parties. They introduced Thomas to many new ideas and areas of study. They talked of many things, including art, navigation, philosophy, politics, natural history, and law.

Once a week Thomas played his violin in a string quartet at the governor's mansion with the governor and two other musicians. Thomas practiced a couple of hours each day and found music to be both stirring and soothing.

Everything interested Thomas. He continued to read many different books and diligently wrote down his thoughts on each subject. He wrote clearly and chose his words with great care. Thomas could hold his own in debates with the older men on nearly any subject. He spent many nights at the governor's mansion in long and serious discussions.

These men talked about the war that was just over. The British had been fighting the French in America, in Europe, and in Asia. The war was called the French and Indian War in America and the Seven Years' War in Britain.

The British had won the war, and the Virginia colonists had celebrated. People on the frontier did not have to worry any longer about Indian attacks led by the French. Many Virginians had fought for the British. One of them was George Washington, who had led other soldiers into many battles. When George Washington came to Williamsburg as a member of the Virginia House of Burgesses, he often went to visit the governor's mansion. Thomas met George there and was in great awe of the military leader.

After he left college at the age of 19, Thomas began to study law in George Wythe's law office. He read law books and wrote many notes about what he read. He regularly went to court with Wythe, and whenever possible he would visit the governor's home to take part in the heated political discussions.

Because he worked for Wythe, Thomas was able to get a seat in the courtroom for a special trial. A **clergyman**, or church minister, had filed a lawsuit against the colony of Virginia. Thomas's old friend Patrick Henry was the lawyer for Virginia. The case was about payment of salary. Through the years, the kings and queens of Britain had ruled that the Church of England was the official church. They paid the salaries of clergymen with money from public taxes. It was the same in the Virginia colony, even though many people had different religions.

The Virginia House of Burgesses had lowered the payment for the clergy. A clergyman asked the British court to change it back. The British court overruled the Virginia House of Burgesses, which made Virginians very angry. This case was to decide how much money Virginia owed the minister for back pay.

Patrick Henry gave a ringing speech, saying that Britain shouldn't throw out laws that the

Thomas's friend, Patrick Henry, was a powerful speaker who also believed that the colonies should be independent.

House of Burgesses made. He said that the clergy were acting unchristian to demand more money. Patrick asked why there was an official church. When he was finished, there was silence in the courtroom. The jury took only a few minutes to decide how much money was owed to the minister: one penny. People in the courtroom went wild, shouting and cheering. They carried Patrick Henry out into the street on their shoulders.

Thomas had watched his friend win the case. He knew that Patrick's fiery speech had helped him win. But was the law on his side, too? Thomas read British law books. He found there was no law that tied the government to a certain religion. The king couldn't tell people what church to belong to. Patrick Henry's claim, that freedom to choose a religion is a natural right of man, was also a legal claim.

Thomas believed there were more privileges that had been wrongly taken away from the people and given to the king. He talked it over with Patrick Henry, and the two agreed that there were many natural rights of man. Another one of those rights, they argued, was for people to have a voice in their own government.

Thomas Jefferson had the nickname "Long Tom" because he was over six feet tall. He was shy and soft-spoken and did not like to talk in public. So he wrote instead.

3

Changing Times

While he studied law, Thomas spent part of his time in Williamsburg and part of his time at Shadwell. No matter where he was, he got out of bed every morning before the sun rose. To wake up, he placed his feet in a bucket of cold water. He had lots to do. From the time he woke up until eight o'clock in the morning he read about scientific subjects. He wanted to learn about animals, plants, and chemistry. From eight until noon, he read law. For the next hour he read about politics.

Thomas thought a learned man should know about many things. He wrote notes about everything he read in his *Commonplace Book*. Here he jotted down legal questions and the movement of planets. Whatever was in his mind, he would write it down clearly and use words precisely.

During the afternoon and evening, he read history and literature and practiced his violin. These were also the times he spent with friends or running Shadwell. He was a very busy man.

Often Thomas's friend Dabney Carr came to Shadwell to visit. The two young men talked about law and rode horses. Dabney got to know Thomas's sister, Martha, and they became very good friends. Before long, Martha and Dabney were married. Now Thomas's best friend was also his brother-in-law.

While Thomas was studying to be a lawyer, the **British Parliament** passed a law called the Sugar Act of 1764. The act claimed that if colonists bought sugar from other countries besides Britain, they had to pay a very high tax. This law didn't bother most Virginians, who traded in tobacco, not sugar. But Thomas was upset by the words in the law because it said that Britain could tax the colonies.

Was he reading too much into the law? No, he decided. It was in legal words, and the meaning was clear. Thomas felt that only the Virginia House of Burgesses had the right to decide what taxes Virginians would pay. Wasn't having a voice in government a natural right of man?

In Williamsburg, meeting at the Raleigh Tavern, Thomas and his friends talked about the tax and what it meant. Virginians elected burgesses to represent them. If a burgess made bad laws or raised taxes unfairly, the voters could vote him out of the House of Burgesses. But Virginians did not elect anyone in the British Parliament to represent them. Virginians could not vote a member out of the British Parliament. If the British Parliament passed a law to make Virginians pay taxes, this would be taxation without representation. The people would not have a voice in the government. Thomas felt this was not right.

Thomas heard rumors that were spreading throughout Virginia. Britain had borrowed lots of money to fight France in the long war. Now the war was over and the British were going to tax the colonists to pay off the borrowed money. After all, they had fought the French and Indians in North America to make the colonists safe. Some people said the British were going to keep a lot of soldiers in the colonies. The soldiers had to be paid. Britain also wanted to collect more taxes from the colonists to pay their soldiers.

Thomas thought Virginians should make their own laws about taxes. They should run their own colony without Britain telling them what to do. Was the Sugar Act just the beginning? Would Britain place more taxes on the colonists? Thomas thought it would. And he was right. The British Parliament passed the Stamp Act of 1765. It made all paper documents need a British stamp to make them legal. Wills, birth certificates, and marriage licenses needed stamps. Newspapers also needed stamps. Other

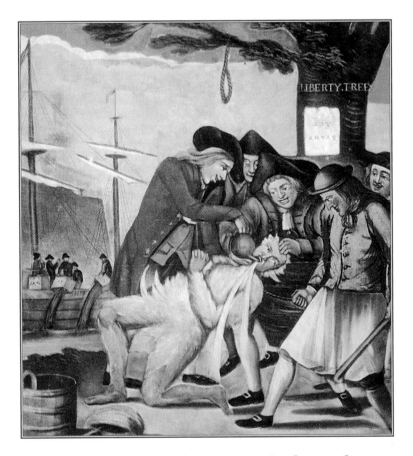

This is a British cartoon. It shows the Bostonians protesting the Stamp Act by pouring tea down the throat of a tarred and feathered stamp tax collector.

items for sale, such as playing cards and dice, needed stamps.

Lawyers were angry. Newspaper owners were angry. Tradesmen were very angry. Some people rioted. In some colonies the stamp tax collectors were caught by the outraged people. The tax collectors were covered with sticky tar and feathers and driven out of town.

In the Virginia House of Burgesses, the lawmakers wrote a **petition** to the king of Britain asking that the Stamp Act not be a law. The petition was not strong enough for Patrick Henry, who was now a burgess. Thomas stood in the capitol lobby by the door to the large meeting room. Because he was not a burgess, he could not go inside the room. But he listened while his friend Patrick spoke his mind.

Patrick Henry said Virginians had certain natural rights. These were the rights that he and Thomas had talked about on many occasions. One of these rights was that Virginians could make their own laws without Britain telling them what to do. Patrick Henry even made a rude remark about the king of Britain. Thomas Jefferson agreed with him. However, some men in the capitol were stunned by Patrick's words.

Patrick Henry gestures dramatically and raises a fiery voice in the House of Burgesses in strong protest against the Stamp Act.

Besides the Virginians, other colonies were also against the Stamp Act. With all the uproar, Britain finally decided that it would be in its best interests to withdraw the act.

Thomas wanted to be a great speaker like Patrick Henry. He read a book on how to give speeches, and he practiced. But his voice was too soft. He didn't have a dramatic flair. George Wythe, the lawyer he worked for, told him to stick to writing because he was very good at it.

After five years of reading law, Thomas took the law examination in 1767 and passed. Then his routine changed. He took cases in small towns throughout the colony and rode his horse to courts. Many of his clients were poor frontier farmers who paid him in goods instead of money. Thomas stayed with them in their rough cabins and asked many questions about the plants and animals in the area. He always took notes.

Thomas had other clients who were wealthy plantation owners. When he stayed in their huge houses he became fascinated with architecture. Back at Shadwell, he decided to build himself a house. As a site for the building, he picked the special little mountain he and Dabney Carr had climbed so many times. He drew up plans for the house and called it Monticello, which meant "little mountain" in Italian.

Thomas packed every day full of activities. Besides his law practice, he was in charge of Shadwell. He managed the slaves, sold tobacco, oversaw the planting of crops, and balanced the accounting books. Now he added another job to his already long list. He was elected to the Virginia House of Burgesses.

At the capitol in Williamsburg, Thomas was surrounded by many old friends and some very important people. Among the other members of the Virginia House of Burgesses were George Washington, Patrick Henry, and George Wythe.

In Thomas's first session, he introduced a bill to make it easier to free slaves. Even though he owned slaves and knew it would be hard for him to run Shadwell without them, he still was uncomfortable with the idea of slavery. Other plantation owners voted against the bill and defeated it.

Monticello was the beautiful home of Thomas and his family. He designed it himself and oversaw its construction. Wherever he traveled, he was always eager to get back to his home.

The burgesses did agree on one issue. They were all against the new British taxes on glass, lead, tea, and paper. They passed a **resolution** that said Britain could not tax Virginians. They also decided that Virginians should not buy the taxed items. Once again the British Parliament thought it wise to back down. The British removed the tax on all the items except tea.

Back at Shadwell, Thomas was overseeing the building of Monticello. Only one room at Monticello was anywhere near finished when the main house at Shadwell burned down. All of Thomas's precious books were lost, but one of the slaves saved his violin. Now Thomas had to move into Monticello.

Soon Thomas met a charming young lady named Martha Wayles Skelton, who was a widow. The two fell very much in love with each other. Martha also liked music. She played the harpsichord while Thomas played the violin. She was pretty and smart. Martha and Thomas were married on New Year's Day in 1772.

Thomas took his new bride back to the one finished room at Monticello. His life looked sunny. His new house was going up. He and his wife were starting a family. But if he looked east from his safe little mountain, he could see storm clouds of change brewing.

Throughout the colonies, people gathered to form Committees of Correspondence. The committees sent messages back and forth to one another telling each other what the British were doing in each colony.

4

The Declaration of Independence

Thomas Jefferson was happily living the life of a country farmer. He had a beautiful wife and a lovely new baby daughter. He was building a magnificent new house for his cherished family which he filled with the many gadgets he invented. Thomas designed gardens and planted new crops.

With all of these activities, Thomas still spent a lot of time reading. He read about agriculture and architecture and sent away for books on revolutions and wars. He read about government and sorted out his thoughts on Britain and the colonies.

The British Parliament had just passed another

law that he also disliked. The law said colonists could be taken to Britain for trials. In fact, in the Rhode Island colony there was a case that they were considering taking to Britain. Thomas felt that people should be judged by a jury of others like themselves. British people lived a different type of life than that of American people and therefore could not give colonists from Rhode Island a fair trial.

Most of the news from Rhode Island reached Virginia through newspapers which the British governor had to approve. Were the newspapers printing the truth? Or were they printing what the British governor wanted them to print? How could Thomas and other Virginians know how the people in Rhode Island really felt about the trial law?

In March 1773 Thomas met with some of the younger members of the House of Burgesses at Raleigh Tavern. They discussed the new British trial law. They decided to form a **Committee of Correspondence** that would be responsible for writing letters to the other colonies. They would find out from the letters what the British were doing in those colonies.

Dabney Carr, Thomas's best friend, presented their idea to the House of Burgesses. It was approved, and a committee was set up to write to the other colonies. Now the real news of how Britain was treating all of the colonies would be known very quickly by everyone.

A few weeks after his speech, Dabney Carr got sick and died. He was buried before Thomas could get back to Monticello. Remembering their boyhood promise to each other, Thomas had Dabney's coffin dug up and placed in a grave under the big oak tree where they had sat so often as boys.

Martha's father died 12 days after Dabney's death, and she inherited 11,000 acres of land and 135 slaves. The Jeffersons sold most of the land but kept the slaves, including light-skinned Betty Hemmings and her little daughter, Sally.

Thomas wrote many letters to find out what

was happening in the other colonies. Through the Committee of Correspondence, he learned about the Boston Tea Party not long after it occurred in December 1773. In Boston, ships filled with tea arrived from Britain. The price of tea was very cheap, but part of the price was a tax. People from Boston refused to buy the tea. They would not pay the tax. Men from Boston dressed up as Indians and threw the tea over the sides of ships into the water.

Thomas and some other members of the House of Burgesses were discussing this in a meeting when a letter arrived. The letter said the British Parliament had just passed a law to close the port of Boston. It was a punishment for the men dumping the tea overboard. The port would be closed on June 1, 1774.

The Virginians were stunned. Boston would be hurt very badly by the British not allowing ships in or out of the harbor. Thomas came up with a brilliant idea. All the people of Virginia should dress in black and pray and not eat on

Angry colonists in Boston disguised themselves as Indians and dumped many boxes of British tea into Boston Harbor.

June 1st. All the businesses should close on that day too. This would show the English king that Virginians supported Boston.

The House of Burgesses passed Thomas's resolution. When the British governor heard of it, he closed the capitol. Thomas and other members didn't go home, however. They went to the Raleigh Tavern and talked. They decided to write to other colonies and ask them to send **delegates** to a meeting of all the colonies. They would call it the **Continental Congress**. The delegates could meet in September and decide how to deal with Britain.

Thomas went back to Monticello and thought about how the British were treating the colonies. He wrote a paper about the rights of the British and the rights of the colonists. He wrote that Britain should not make laws for the American colonies. He made two copies of his paper and then left for Williamsburg to present it to the delegates of the Continental Congress.

On the way to Williamsburg, Thomas got sick and had to return home. He sent copies of his paper to Patrick Henry and to the speaker of the House of Burgesses. Thomas's statement was read to the delegates. Many cheered. Others thought it was too bold. Later, a revised, softer proposal was sent to the Continental Congress.

Thomas's friends had the paper printed as a

pamphlet, and hundreds of copies were sent around to all of the colonies. It wasn't very long before some copies showed up in Britain too. Now many people knew Thomas Jefferson's name. They knew he had good ideas and that he was a good writer.

At Monticello, Thomas read letters about the congress. Twelve colonies had sent delegates. They decided to stop trading with Britain. Thomas knew the formation of the congress was the first step in uniting the colonies. He believed that the colonists should not think of themselves as Virginians or New Yorkers but, rather, as Americans.

In March 1775 Thomas attended Virginia's convention. He was as spellbound as other members when Patrick Henry rose to his feet and asked that Virginia raise a **militia**. They needed armed men to protect the colony. The members voted in favor of Patrick's radical idea. Thomas knew that raising a Virginia army could mean there would be a war with Britain.

He was right. A few weeks later, fighting broke out in Massachusetts. Shots were fired between British soldiers and the Massachusetts militia at Lexington and Concord, and men were killed. The king sent an urgent message to the governors of the colonies. The Virginia governor called the House of Burgesses together to give them the message. It said that Britain would not tax the colonies for now.

That was not enough for Thomas. He didn't want Britain to make any laws for the colonies. So he wrote a very strong reply. The members liked his reply and sent Thomas to Philadelphia to deliver it to the Continental Congress.

In June 1775, when Thomas made his journey to Pennsylvania, the Continental Congress was setting up a government of the colonies. The Continental Congress also organized an army of colonists and put George Washington in charge of it. While in Philadelphia, Thomas met many famous leaders from the other colonies. He met Benjamin Franklin of Pennsylvania, as well as

British soldiers and American colonists fire shots at one another at the Battle of Concord. This battle marked the beginning of the American Revolutionary War.

John Adams and John Hancock of Massachusetts.

Thomas read his reply to Britain out loud to the members of the congress. Leaders from some of the colonies thought it was too strong. So after much discussion and debate, the congress passed a weaker version of Thomas's reply.

In August 1775, Thomas returned home to Monticello, the place he loved best. However, things were not gong well at home. His second daughter died soon after his return. His mother was ill, and his wife was also sick. Thomas was very sad, but the congress was meeting and he had to leave for Philadelphia in September. When it let out for winter break, he once again went home.

Thomas's little mountain was not a happy place anymore. His wife was still very sick, and his mother was growing weaker by the day. Soon his mother died. Thomas was filled with grief and began suffering terrible headaches. He took long, lonely horseback rides across his land.

While he was feeling so sad, a friend sent him a pamphlet, *Common Sense*, by Thomas Paine. Thomas read it again and again. Finally a writer had called the king a **tyrant**! In the pamphlet, Thomas read how Paine wanted the colonists to be free of Britain's rule. Thomas had already thought of this himself. Now, seeing it in writing, he was ready to act on it. So were many others.

In the spring, Thomas once again went back to Philadelphia to be a part of the Continental Congress. Many members wanted independence from Britain. On June 7, Richard Henry Lee of Virginia read a resolution. It called for no rule by Britain and for free states. In no uncertain terms, it called for independence.

The leaders talked about the resolution. They decided to wait until July to vote on it. By then delegates could find out what the people in their colonies wanted to do. If Congress voted for liberty, a declaration of independence should be ready. A committee was set up to write it. Thomas Jefferson, Benjamin Franklin, John Adams, Roger Sherman, and Robert R. Livingston met, talked about their ideas, and discussed how to best proceed.

The committee finally decided that only one man should write the declaration. They chose the best writer–Thomas Jefferson.

The Declaration of Independence as Thomas wrote it is preserved so that all Americans may see it. Thomas wrote the document on a portable desk that he had invented.

The New Nation

Thomas bent over the writing desk. He tapped the feather of his quill pen against his forehead and searched his mind for the right word. He wrote "liberty."

He had written many papers in his life. But none was as important as the one he worked on during the hot June days of 1776. The Declaration of Independence had to be his best writing. It would tell the world why the American colonies must be free from British rule.

Thomas wrote down words, words, and more words, and then he crossed them out and started again. This had to be exactly right. He had prepared all of his 33 years to write this document. His time studying at the College of William and Mary, his time reading the law, and his time serving in the House of Burgesses all were for this moment.

For 17 days he worked on the Declaration of Independence and then submitted a draft. First the committee reviewed it. Then the Continental Congress read it. Only a few words and phrases were changed. The members took out a section against slavery. On July 4, 1776, they voted in favor of independence from Britain. They voted to form a new nation.

Copies were made of the document, and they were sent to all of the colonies. When the declaration was read to a crowd gathered in Philadelphia, the people

> "We hold these truths to be self-evident, that all men are created equal, that they are endowed by their Creator with certain inalienable Rights, that among these are Life, Liberty and the Pursuit of Happiness."
>
> —Thomas Jefferson
> From the Declaration
> of Independence

**Citizens of Boston cheer and wave as
the Declaration of Independence is
read aloud to them.**

cheered. They lit bonfires and set off fireworks
in celebration. A copy was read to Washington's
army. The soldiers now knew what they were

fighting for. They were fighting for personal freedom, for a new nation where all men were created equal.

Thomas had only been in Philadelphia for a few short months, but they were very busy months. Now he wanted to get back to his family at Monticello. Just as soon as another Virginia delegate arrived to replace him, he went home.

While Thomas was at the congress, Virginia had elected Patrick Henry as governor. The House of Burgesses had become the House of Delegates, and members had been writing a new **constitution** for the state. Thomas had his own ideas for the new system of government.

In the northern states, the American army fought many difficult battles with the British soldiers. Thomas stayed in Virginia and wrote new laws for the next three years. He worked hard to get delegates to pass the new laws. One of the the most important laws Thomas worked on was about religion.

Under Britain's rule the colonists paid taxes to the Church of England, even if they didn't belong to the church. Thomas said that a person had a right to choose his own religion. He said that a person's religious ideas did not rob or hurt anyone else. His religion was his own business. There should be no religion supported by taxes. Thomas also wanted public education for children. He thought educated people would work to keep their freedoms.

In June 1779 Thomas was elected governor of Virginia. British soldiers had already invaded his state. Thomas was in charge of raising money and supplies for the militia.

The House of Delegates moved up the James River from Williamsburg to Richmond. They thought it would be safer there. But the British soldiers came up the river too. The delegates moved again, this time to Charlottesville, just four miles away from Monticello. Some of the delegates stayed at Thomas's home with the Jefferson family.

Early one morning, a militia captain rode up to Monticello. He warned Thomas that the British were coming and that the soldiers were only a few hours behind him. Thomas sent his family away to safety and then called an emergency meeting of the delegates. After the meeting, the delegates fled to their homes.

Thomas burned some official papers and took others with him. He left his house only minutes before the British came. The soldiers stole his wine and drank it, but they did not harm Monticello.

Thomas did not like being governor and was glad when his term was over. He said he was not prepared to be a military leader of a state. He decided to stay out of politics.

After years of war, with victories and defeats, the Americans defeated the British at Yorktown, Virginia, in October 1781. As this battle, the last big battle of the war, was being fought, Thomas was working on a book. He had been asked by a Frenchman to write about his state. Thomas

General George Washington accepts the surrender of the defeated British army at Yorktown, Virginia, after winning the final major battle of the war.

wrote in great detail about Virginia's land, plants, animals, history, and culture. He called it *Notes on the State of Virginia.*

While he worked on this book, his wife's health got worse. Three of their five children had died. After giving birth to their sixth child in 1782, Martha became extremely weak. Thomas stayed close by and nursed her tenderly, but, sadly, Martha Jefferson never recovered. She died on September 6, 1782. Thomas recorded the day his wife died in his journal as the worst day of his life. He stayed in his room for weeks, sick with grief. Then he rode his horse over the hills and into the woods on his land. He remembered good times with Martha. Sometimes he smiled. Sometimes he cried. He gained strength to face bad times and go on living.

After Martha's death, Thomas went back into politics. Virginia elected him to the Continental Congress. Two of his ideas shaped the new nation. He had a plan to make new states out of the Northwest Territory, the land west of the Appalachian Mountains and east of the Mississippi River. He also had a plan for American money that was based on the number 10, dividing a dollar into 100 pennies or 10 dimes.

In May 1784 the Congress asked Thomas to go on an important mission to Paris, France, to make trade treaties with some of the European

**The Treaty of Paris, which officially
ended the war between America and
Britain, was signed in Paris, France.**

countries. Benjamin Franklin and John Adams
were already working on the treaties there.
Thomas left his two youngest daughters with

relatives but took his oldest daughter to France with him. She attended school there while Thomas met with important European leaders.

Thomas loved Paris. He especially liked the old buildings and the bookstores. He talked to many of the people and learned about their lives. While he was in Paris, Thomas read many new books and continued taking lengthy notes. He sent many different plants, birds, trees, and animals back to Monticello and traveled to several other European countries.

He was happy for a while, but not for long. Thomas soon learned that his youngest daughter had also died. Now he wanted his other surviving daughter to be with him. Sally Hemmings, the 14-year-old slave, traveled with her across the

Thomas had seen many different hot air balloons while in France. Also, with President George Washington, he watched a balloon take off from Philadelphia in 1793. While in Philadelphia, Thomas wrote home to his daughter that he wished he had one. Then, instead of taking 10 days to get home, he could make the trip in a balloon in five hours.

wide and dangerous ocean to France.

While Thomas was still in France, leaders in the United States wrote a new constitution. It set up a new government for America. Thomas sent many books on government and freedom to his friend James Madison. Thomas wanted his ideas in the new constitution. James Madison was sure to put Thomas's idea about freedom of religion in the list of the rights of the people.

After five years in France, as a civil war was breaking out, Thomas and his two daughters boarded a ship to return home and to a new nation—the United States of America.

Thomas served the new nation as a great statesman. He was the first secretary of state, the
second vice president, and the third president
of the United States.

6

American Statesman

George Washington was elected the first president of the United States of America under the new constitution. Washington asked Thomas Jefferson to be the first secretary of state.

Thomas accepted the position, and when he reported to work, he found that he had many very different jobs, including taking care of business with other countries and being in charge of Indian affairs, weights and measures, and patents for inventions.

Sometimes Thomas disagreed with the secretary of the treasury, Alexander Hamilton. Although both men worked for the good of the country, they had different opinions on how strong the central government should be.

In 1793 Thomas resigned as secretary of state and went home to Monticello. He rebuilt the main house to three times its original size and wrote many letters to friends in the government.

When John Adams became the second president, Thomas was sworn in as his vice president. Thomas was also elected as the new president of a scientific and philosophical group. He showed this group a skeleton of a giant sloth that was found in a Virginia cave. He had written a scientific paper about the sloth, which he read to the group members.

In 1801 Thomas Jefferson was elected the third president of the United States. He had a very different style from the first two presidents. Instead of riding in a carriage, he walked to the unfinished capitol in Washington, D.C. There he was sworn in. He gave a very good speech. Unfortunately, only the first few rows of people could hear it. Thomas still hated speaking in public, and his voice was still very soft.

Thomas moved into the new president's house. Unlike Washington and Adams, Thomas did not like big formal parties. He gave small dinners where guests sat at a round table and talked about government, science, and the arts. Thomas also let the public come to the mansion. On the Fourth of July, he held a parade on the lawn and invited people inside for cake, wine, and lemonade.

John Adams and Thomas Jefferson became instant friends when they first met at the Continental Congress. In France they were often dinner companions. Although they had a falling-out during the 1800 election, years later they became good friends again. They wrote hundreds of letters to each other. Both men died on July 4, 1826.

As president, Thomas was faced with big problems with other countries. For example, pirates in Tripoli, in northern Africa, made American ships pay money to safely use the sea. Thomas said America would not pay. He sent warships to fight the pirates. Finally, America reached a peace agreement with Tripoli.

Also, Spain had secretly given France the land from the Mississippi River to the Rocky Mountains. France also owned New Orleans at the mouth of that big river. If France ever closed the river to American ships, Americans wouldn't have a way of getting their goods to market.

Thomas offered to buy New Orleans. The French leader, Napoleon, said no. But he would sell all of the Louisiana Territory for $15 million. Thomas agreed and got the Congress to agree too. For about three cents an acre, Thomas had doubled the size of the nation. The Louisiana Purchase of 1803 added over 800,000 square miles to U. S. territory.

Most of this area was not mapped yet. Earlier, Thomas had asked Meriwether Lewis and William Clark to explore the area. They were to make a detailed report about what they found. Their **expedition** set out in 1804. They carried medals with Thomas Jefferson's picture on one side and a picture of a Native American and a white man clasping hands on the other side.

Lewis and Clark gave these medals to Indian chiefs as gifts for peace and friendship.

Thomas was elected president for a second term. During his second term in office, Lewis and Clark returned from their long trip. They brought back plants, animals, maps of rivers, and even Indians.

After Thomas had been president for eight years, he rode out of Washington, D.C., and never returned. He went back to his beloved Monticello. Many friends visited him there and at times there were as many as 50 guests in the 35-room mansion. Some stayed several weeks, and some stayed several months.

Thomas's most trusted house slave, Sally Hemmings, kept his private rooms in order. Besides visiting with friends, Thomas read his books, rode his horse, and wrote letters. Then he started another big project.

Thomas believed that education was important to a free nation. He convinced Virginia lawmakers to build the University of Virginia in

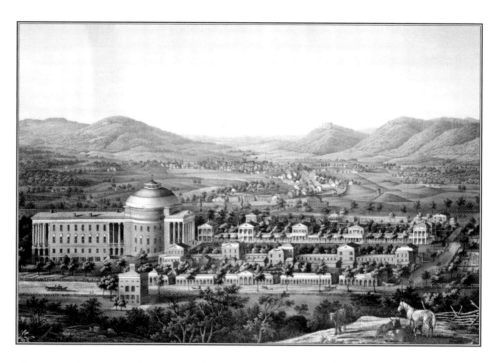

Among Thomas's many interests was architecture. He designed and drew up the plans for the University of Virginia, the first university to be started by a state.

Charlottesville. It was the first university in the nation that was started by a state and not by a religious group. Thomas laid out the grounds and designed the buildings. Some days, when he couldn't ride the four miles to Charlottesville to oversee the construction, he watched the work through a telescope from Monticello.

When the first students came to the new

university, Thomas invited them to dinner, and several times a week thereafter he entertained students at Monticello. He remembered his days as a student when he had learned so much from Professor William Small, lawyer George Wythe, and Governor Francis Fauquier. Thomas told the students about the beginning of the new nation and shared his ideas for the country.

The upkeep of Monticello had used up most of Thomas's money. To pay some of his debts, he sold many of his books to the Congress. Around 10,000 of his books became the foundation for the Library of Congress.

Although he needed money, he began buying more books saying that he could not live without them. He was in danger of having to sell Monticello. People across the country learned that Thomas needed money, and many started sending it to him. With the assistance of many people's donations, he kept Monticello.

In the summer of 1826, Thomas fell ill. He knew he was dying, but he wanted to live until the one day that meant so much to him and the country. On the third of July he asked his doctor if it was the fourth. Just a few more hours, he was told.

The Fourth of July dawned bright. Across the nation guns sounded, soldiers marched, and flags flew high. Fifty years earlier, the nation had been born.

That afternoon, Thomas Jefferson died.

On his desk, he had left a drawing of his tombstone. He wanted the most important things he had done written on it:

> Here was buried, Thomas Jefferson, Author
> of the Declaration of American Independence,
> of the Statute of Virginia for religious free-
> dom, & Father of The University of Virginia.

He was buried under that special sprawling oak tree at Monticello near his wife and his best friend, Dabney Carr. In his will, he freed five slaves and all members of Sally Hemmings's family. His date of birth is not remembered by

Americans celebrate their freedom from British rule by putting up a liberty pole on the Fourth of July in honor of the Declaration of Independence.

the country he loved. But his date of death is celebrated as Thomas would have wanted it– with parades, picnics, and fireworks.

GLOSSARY

British Parliament–a group of men in Britain who make laws

clergyman–minister

colony–an area controlled by a distant nation

Committee of Correspondence–a group of men who wrote to people in other colonies

constitution–a set of principles

Continental Congress–a group of men elected from all colonies to decide policies

delegate–a person who represents others

expedition–a journey for a certain purpose

House of Burgesses–elected group of men who made the laws of Virginia

militia–a group of civilian men called into the military only during emergencies

petition–a formal request

plantation–an estate with a very large farm that usually harvests one main crop

resolution–a formal statement

surveyor–a person whose job is to measure the land

tyrant–a highly controlling ruler

CHRONOLOGY

1743 Thomas Jefferson born on April 13 at Shadwell Plantation, Virginia.

1760 Enters the College of William and Mary in Williamsburg, Virginia.

1768 Elected to Virginia House of Burgesses.

1769 Begins building his home, Monticello.

1772 Marries Martha Wayles Skelton on January 1.

1776 Writes the Declaration of Independence from June 11–28; on July 4th the congress adopts the Declaration of Independence.

1779–81 Serves as governor of Virginia.

1782 His wife, Martha, dies.

1784–89 Serves as special ambassador in France.

1790 Appointed first secretary of state of the United States.

1797 Elected vice president of the United States.

1801 Elected third president of the United States; serves for two terms.

1809 Retires to Monticello.

1826 Attends the opening of the University of Virginia; dies on the 4th of July at Monticello at age 83.

REVOLUTIONARY WAR TIME LINE ═══

1765 The Stamp Act is passed by the British. Violent protests against it break out in the colonies.

1766 Britain ends the Stamp Act.

1767 Britain passes a law that taxes glass, painter's lead, paper, and tea in the colonies.

1770 Five colonists are killed by British soldiers in the Boston Massacre.

1773 People are angry about the taxes on tea. They throw boxes of tea from ships in Boston harbor into the water. It ruins the tea. The event is called the Boston Tea Party.

1774 The British pass laws to punish Boston for the Boston Tea Party. They close Boston harbor. Leaders in the colonies meet to plan a response to these actions.

1775 The battles of Lexington and Concord begin the American Revolution.

1776 The Declaration of Independence is signed. France and Spain give money to help the Americans fight Britain. Nathan Hale is captured by the British. He is charged with being a spy and is executed.

1777 Leaders choose a flag for America. The American troops win some important battles over the British. General Washington and his troops spend a very cold, hungry winter in Valley Forge.

1778 France sends ships to help the Americans win the war. The British are forced to leave Philadelphia.

1779 French ships head back to France. The French support the Americans in other ways.

1780 Americans discover that Benedict Arnold is a traitor. He escapes to the British. Major battles take place in North and South Carolina.

1781 The British surrender at Yorktown.

1783 A peace treaty is signed in France. British troops leave New York.

1787 The U.S. Constitution is written. Delaware becomes the first state in the Union.

1789 George Washington becomes the first president. John Adams is vice president.

FURTHER READING

Colver, Anne. *Thomas Jefferson: Author of Independence*. Philadelphia: Chelsea House, 1992.

Fisher, Leonard Everett. *Monticello*. New York: Holiday House, 1988.

Giblin, James Cross. *Thomas Jefferson*. New York: Scholastic, 1994.

Greene, Carol. *Thomas Jefferson: Author, Inventor, President*. Danbury, CT: Children's Press, 1991.

Morris, Jeffrey Brandon. *The Jefferson Way*. Minneapolis: Lerner Publications, 1994.

Old, Wendie C. *Thomas Jefferson*. Springfield, NJ: Enslow Publishers, 1997.

Severance, John B. *Thomas Jefferson: Architect of Democracy*. New York: Clarion Books, 1998.

Usel, T.M. *Thomas Jefferson*. Danbury, CT: Children's Press, 1996.

PICTURE CREDITS

INDEX

ABOUT THE AUTHOR

Award-winning writer **VEDA BOYD JONES** enjoys the challenge of writing for a variety of readers. Her published works include nine adult novels, four children's historical novels, six children's biographies, a coloring book, and numerous articles and short stories in national magazines. In addition to working at her computer, she teaches writing and speaks at writers' conferences. Mrs. Jones lives in the Missouri Ozarks with her husband, Jimmie, and three sons, Landon, Morgan, and Marshall.

Senior Consulting Editor **ARTHUR M. SCHLESINGER, JR.** is the leading American historian of our time. He won the Pulitzer Prize for his book *The Age of Jackson* (1945), and again for *A Thousand Days* (1965). This chronicle of the Kennedy Administration also won a National Book Award. He has written many other books, including a multi-volume series, *The Age of Roosevelt*. Professor Schlesinger is the Albert Schweitzer Professor of the Humanities at the City University of New York, and has been involved in several other Chelsea House projects, including the Colonial Leaders series of biographies on the most prominent figures of early American history.